EASY

BATIK

LANDSCAPE QUILTS

PAT BROWN

American Quilter's Society
P.O. Box 3290 • Paducah, KY 42002-3290
www.AmericanQuilter.com

Located in Paducah, Kentucky, the American Quilter's Society (AQS) is dedicated to promoting the accomplishments of today's quilters. Through its publications and events, AQS strives to honor today's quiltmakers and their work and to inspire future creativity and innovation in quiltmaking.

EXECUTIVE BOOK EDITOR: ANDI MILAM REYNOLDS
SENIOR EDITOR: LINDA BAXTER LASCO
COPY EDITOR: CHRYSTAL ABHALTER
GRAPHIC DESIGN: ELAINE WILSON
ILLUSTRATIONS: MELISSA POTTERBAUM
COVER DESIGN: MICHAEL BUCKINGHAM
QUILT PHOTOGRAPHY: CHARLES R. LYNCH
ROOM PHOTOGRAPHY: BRYCE AND SAVANNA BROWN

ATTENTION PHOTOCOPYING SERVICE: Please note the following — Publisher and author give permission to print page 35 for personal use only.

Additional copies of this book may be ordered from the American Quilter's Society, PO Box 3290, Paducah, KY 42002-3290, or online at www.AmericanQuilter.com.

Text © 2011, Author, Patricia L. Brown
Artwork © 2011, American Quilter's Society

LIBRARY OF CONGRESS CATALOGING-IN-PUBLICATION DATA

Brown, Patricia L. (Patricia Lee), 1951-
  Easy batik landscape quilts / by Patricia L. Brown.
    p. cm.
  ISBN 978-1-60460-004-9
  1. Patchwork--Patterns. 2. Quilting--Patterns. 3. Batik. 4. Fabric pictures. 5. Landscapes in art. I. Title.
  TT835.B73118 2011
  746.46'041--dc23
                           2011035692

PREVIOUS PAGE FEATURED QUILT: PERFECT ENDING. Instructions begin on page 70.

DEDICATED TO

My husband, who is truly
my best friend and biggest fan;

My sons and daughters-in-law;

And my beloved grandchildren;

All of whom make it a joy to live
each day on God's beautiful earth.

ACKNOWLEDGMENT

I would like to give special
thanks to my son, Bryce, and his
wife, Savanna, for all the time
and effort they put into the home
decorating photos in this book.

FEATURED QUILT: TUSCAN MORNING. Instructions begin on
page 56.

PREFACE

I am convinced that every room in every home has a mood. These moods can be manipulated from mind-numbing dreary and depressing to joyful and uplifting just by changing what's on the walls.

I am a big fan of every home having lots of quilts, as the unique colors and textures give off a feeling that only textiles can. With the proper lighting, the quilting on a quilt can have as much "wow" factor as the actual colors and patterns used in the quilt.

So let's pursue the goal that quilters might see the opportunity of a small change making a big difference in the mood and personality of their living spaces. Even in a cramped office cubicle, a tiny piece of quilted art can make you feel better every time you glance that way. To me, just to touch the texture of a finely quilted piece has a magical, comforting feeling.

I hope the inspiration of my own quilts might, with little effort or money, completely change your spaces to make room for more joy!

FEATURED QUILT: COUNTRY LIGHTS. Instructions begin on page 64.

CONTENTS

INTRODUCTION 6

GENERAL INSTRUCTIONS 8

LANDSCAPE PROJECTS 12

Mountains 12
   GOLDEN EVENING 12
   NIGHT RAIN COMING 16
   MOUNTAIN SPRING 20
   DREAM TIME 24
   NIGHT SENTINEL 28

Moons 32
   NIGHT DANCE 32
   NIGHTFALL...BE VERY CAREFUL . . . 36
   TOUCH OF DEW 40
   SEA MOON 44
   STAR LIGHT...STAR BRIGHT 48

Moods 52
   DESERT MAN 52
   TUSCAN MORNING 56
   TROPICAL MORNING 60
   COUNTRY LIGHTS/CITY LIGHTS . . . 64
   WINDING PATH 67
   PERFECT ENDING 70

GALLERY 74

QUILTING SUGGESTIONS 78

ABOUT THE AUTHOR 79

INTRODUCTION

My mind operates in "art mode." Every time I enter a new room, while trying my best to concentrate on what the person with me is saying, I am discreetly (I hope) scoping out the area for eye-catching vignettes and beautiful color combinations.

There is nothing like nature to draw inspiration from. I hope to inspire all levels of quilters to do just that!

Nature has incredible mood swings and I especially love to witness them as much as possible...unless lightning is involved! Then I don't care how beautiful nature is. I am the first one out of the area!

Batiks are used a great deal in creating these naturescapes as they present a feeling as only a batik fabric can. With the unique color combinations, swirls, and patterns, they can give the effect of an actual glow and/or movement.

You will notice that the mountains, foliage, etc., in these quilts are cut freehand. Now don't panic! If you can draw a curving line, you can make these basic patterns. The

Featured quilt: Desert Man. Instructions begin on page 52.

thing that is great about freehand cutting is that you really can't make a mistake. Just study the pattern assembly diagram and start to fill in the pattern in actual size on graph paper. You might want to use a pencil for obvious reasons!

I personally still only hand quilt as I feel I can make a bigger statement with the patterns of the quilting. I've included quilting suggestions (page 78). If you make straight line moonbeams or sunbeams radiating from the moon or sun, it gives them an extra dimension. I use a lot of straight-line quilting, with a yardstick as my marking tool.

Your own unique wall quilts are great conversation starters as people are almost always interested in something unusual. If nothing else, they are curious as to why we would take whole fabric, cut it up into tiny pieces, and then put it back together again! Well, quilters know why and that's what is important.

Landscape depiction is a favorite of mine. There is just something about a mountain and a moon....

GENERAL INSTRUCTIONS

These are free and easy projects. You can alter the dimensions as you please. *The measurements on the patterns are meant simply as proportional guidelines for when you are drawing in the lines for your own project.*

Most of the patterns can be broken down into panels and strips. Any one of the sections can be broken up into smaller components and pieced. It is important to make a full-size pattern, either for the entire quilt or just for the pieced panels—your choice.

YOU GET TO DECIDE!

Determine the size you want to make your quilt and tape together as many sheets of 1" grid graph paper as needed for the size of your project—8½" x 11" or the larger 17" x 22" sheets to make the job easier. Mark off the panels and strips, again using the measurements on the pattern as a guide to the proportion of the pieces as they relate to one another. Use a straightedge such as a long rotary ruler or yardstick to mark the lines.

FEATURED QUILTS, RIGHT: NIGHTFALL…BE VERY CAREFUL. Instructions begin on page 36.

FAR RIGHT: SANTA FE NIGHT. Instructions not included.

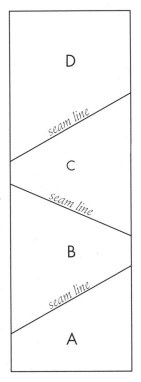

Panel piecing diagram, each section labeled with a letter

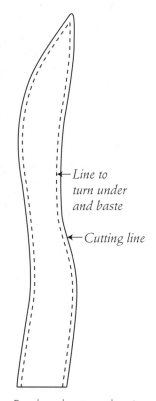

Freehand cut appliqué

The great thing is that you don't have to be exact in the markings at all. The quilts all have a contemporary look, so "close" to the pattern diagram is good enough.

PIECED PANELS

Some of the panels involve basic piecing. Let's assume your pattern includes a panel like this one shown at the left.

After you have made the full-size pattern, cut out each panel section—A, B, C, and D. Lay each section face down on the wrong side of the appropriate fabric. Trace around all four sides with a marker and cut out each section ¼" away from the marked line. Alternatively, you can use a rotary ruler, aligning the ¼" mark with the edges of the pattern and cutting out the fabric with a rotary cutter.

Sew the sections together on the marked lines or, if you've rotary-cut the fabric, with a ¼" seam allowance, right sides together. For this panel, start by joining sections A & B, then join C & D. Join the two sections to complete the panel.

The pieced panel(s) are joined with the plain panels and numbered strips according to the pattern assembly diagrams for each project.

In most cases, appliqués are added after piecing and sewing together the panels and strips. The foliage is cut freehand.

Cut a wavy foliage piece. On the right side of the fabric, mark a ¼" seam allowance along the outside edge of the foliage. Turn under the seam allowance and baste. Appliqué the foliage onto the quilt, positioning it as indicated in the pattern.

Moons and suns on the quilts are made by making a circle pattern. You can use something as simple as the lid from a kitchen pot or a plate that strikes you as the right size. The size is whatever looks good to you. Draw a circle around your "template" on the right side of the fabric. Cut out ¼" beyond the marked line. Turn under on the drawn line and baste. Appliqué the circle onto the quilt according to the appliqué placement diagram.

RIGHT: DREAM TIME, detail. Full quilt on page 25.

LANDSCAPE PROJECTS

Mountains
GOLDEN EVENING

GOLDEN EVENING replicates that rare time of day when all of nature's lighting comes together to make the landscape actually glow! This can be accomplished with fabric by selecting really bright golds and yellows to play off a black sky. Dark foliage in the foreground adds the accent needed to balance the picture of the mountain scene.

RIGHT: GOLDEN EVENING, 57" x 46", made by the author

YARDAGE REQUIREMENTS

Adjust these amounts up or down, depending on whether you decide to make this quilt larger or smaller than the original.

- ▲ 2 yards black for the night sky, sashing strips, and binding
- ▲ ¾ yard EACH of at least 5 coordinating fabrics for the mountains, panel piecing, and moon
- ▲ ¾ yard EACH of 2 foliage fabrics
- ▲ **Backing:** 2¾ yards
- ▲ **Batting:** 61" x 50"

CONSTRUCTION

Determine the finished size of your quilt. Tape together enough sheets of 1" grid graph paper to make a full-size pattern. Use the measurements on the pattern assembly diagram as a guide for drawing the panels and strips.

Cut out the pattern and use the pieces to cut and label your fabrics (letters for the panel sections and numbers for the strips), being sure to add ¼" seam allowance (see General Instructions, pages 8–11).

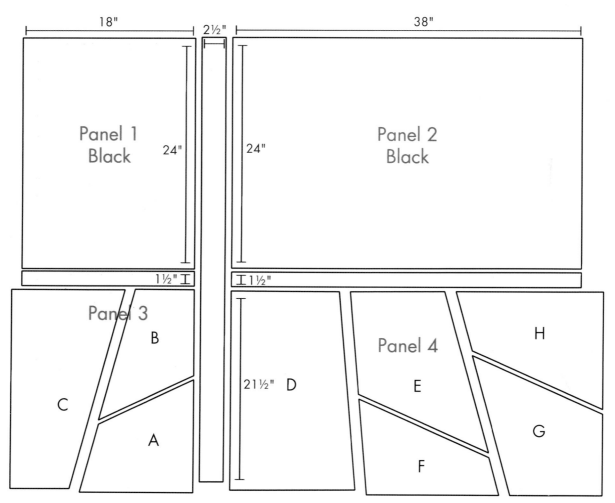

Pattern assembly

For panel 3, piece together sections A & B, then add section C to complete the panel.

For panel 4, join sections E & F, then add D. Join G & H and add to the D/E/F unit to complete the panel.

Join Panel 1, a sashing strip, and Panel 3.

Join Panel 2, a sashing strip, and Panel 4.

Join the two panel units and final sashing strip to complete the top.

APPLIQUÉ AND FINISHING

Freehand draw and cut mountain shapes as shown in the placement diagram.

Layer them as you like and appliqué to the black background.

Draw a circle for the moon on a coordinating fabric and appliqué to the sky background. Freehand cut foliage pieces and appliqué where desired on the quilt.

Quilt as desired and bind your quilt.

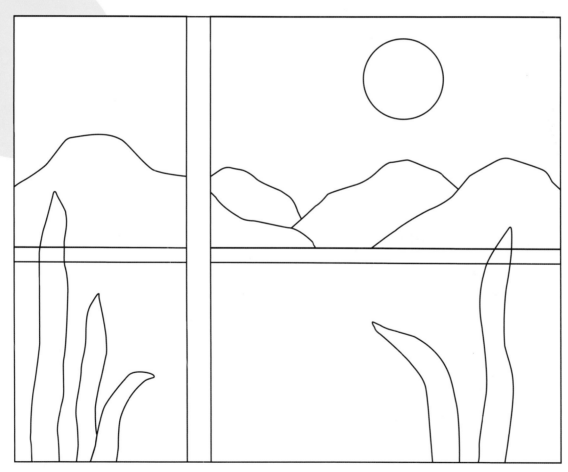

Appliqué placement

EASY BATIK LANDSCAPE QUILTS ▲ PAT BROWN

NIGHT RAIN COMING

By using lots of shades of blues in this quilt and using the gold accents, they combine to cool down the look. The moon isn't going to last for long as the clouds are moving in quickly.

YARDAGE REQUIREMENTS

Adjust these amounts up or down, depending on whether you decide to make this quilt larger or smaller than the original.

- ▲ 1¾ yards black for sky, strips, and binding
- ▲ 1 yard EACH of at least 5 coordinating colors for piecing sections and various strips
- ▲ ¾ yard contrasting fabric for cactus and moon
- ▲ **Backing:** 2¾ yards
- ▲ **Batting:** 60" x 48"

CONSTRUCTION

Determine the finished size of your quilt. Tape together enough sheets of 1" grid graph paper to make a full-size pattern. Use the

LEFT: NIGHT RAIN COMING, 56" x 44", made by the author

measurements on the pattern assembly diagram as a guide for drawing the panels and strips. Note that any of the sections can be divided for piecing.

Cut out the pattern and use the pieces to cut and label your fabrics (letters for the panel sections and numbers for the strips), being sure to add ¼" seam allowance (see General Instructions, pages 8–11).

To make Panel 1, cut 20 squares and sew them together in 5 rows of 4 squares each. Join the rows.

Trace a moon and freehand cut a patch. Appliqué them in place to complete the panel.

Position all the appliqués according to the appliqué placement diagram (page 19).

To make Panel 2, join A & B. Add section C. Join D & E and add to the A/B/C unit.

Trace a moon and appliqué it in place to complete the panel.

Join Panels 1 & 2 and add strip 1 to the bottom of the unit.

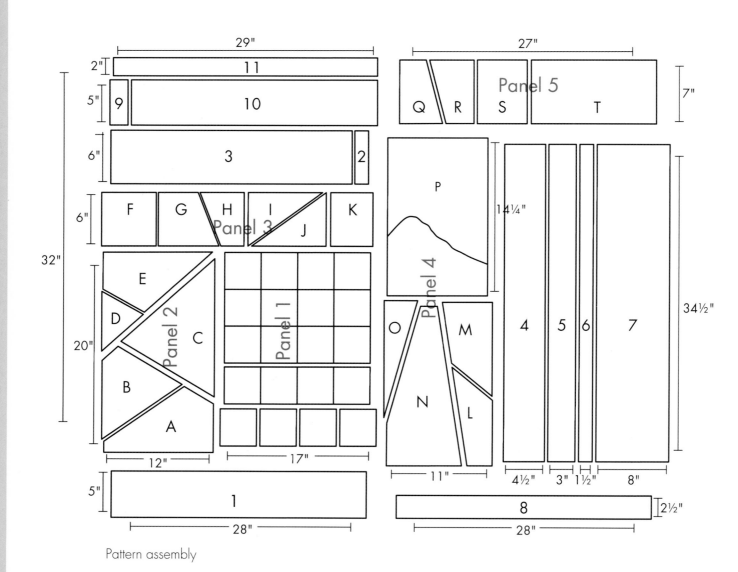

Pattern assembly

Easy Batik Landscape Quilts ▲ Pat Brown

To make Panel 3, join sections F, G & H. Join I & J. Sew the F/G/H unit to the I/J unit. Add the K section to complete the panel.

Join strips 2 & 3.

Freehand draw a mountain and trace a moon. Appliqué them in place. Add the completed strip 2/3 unit to Panel 3.

Join the Panel 3/strip 2/3 unit with the Panel 1/2 unit.

To make Panel 4, join sections L & M, then add sections N and O.

Freehand draw a mountain and trace a moon. Appliqué them to section P. Join the appliquéd section P to the L/M/N/O unit to complete the panel.

Join strips 4, 5, 6 & 7 and add to Panel 4.

Freehand cut a cactus and appliqué it in place. Sew strip 8 to the bottom of Panel 4 and the 4/5/6/7 unit.

Join the completed panel units. Freehand cut a mountain-shaped patch and appliqué to the bottom of the units.

To make Panel 5, join sections Q, R, S & T. Freehand cut a patch and appliqué it in place to complete the panel.

Join strips 9 & 10, then add strip 11. Add to Panel 5, then add the strip and panel unit to the top of the previously joined panels to complete the top.

Quilt as you prefer and bind your quilt.

Appliqué placement

MOUNTAIN SPRING

You can almost smell the fresh mountain air when you look at this quilt. Pastel fabrics bring the mountains to life in a whole different way. The foreground fabrics gently accentuate the colors of the mountains while the foliage frames the foothills.

YARDAGE REQUIREMENTS

Adjust these amounts up or down, depending on whether you decide to make this quilt larger or smaller than the original.

▲ 1¾ yards for sky, top, bottom, side strips, and binding

▲ ¾ yard EACH of at least 8 coordinating fabrics for mountains, foreground, foliage, and moons

▲ 1¾ yards contrasting fabric for top strip

▲ 1⅓ yards for the side strips

▲ ½ yard of 2–3 foliage fabrics

▲ **Backing:** 2½ yards

▲ **Batting:** 59" x 43"

RIGHT: MOUNTAIN SPRING, 55" x 39", made by the author

CONSTRUCTION

Determine the finished size of your quilt. Tape together enough sheets of 1" grid graph paper to make a full-size pattern. Use the measurements on the pattern assembly diagrams as a guide for drawing the panels and strips. Note that any of the sections can be divided for piecing.

Cut out the pattern and use the pieces to cut and label your fabrics (letters for the panel sections and numbers for the strips), being sure to add ¼" seam allowance (see General Instructions, pages 8–11).

Making the Mountains Panel

Join sections A & B, add C, then D. Set aside.

Join sections E & F, add G. Join H & I and add to the E/F/G unit.

Add sections J and K to the E/F/G/H/I unit. Add the A/B/C/D unit to complete the mountain panel.

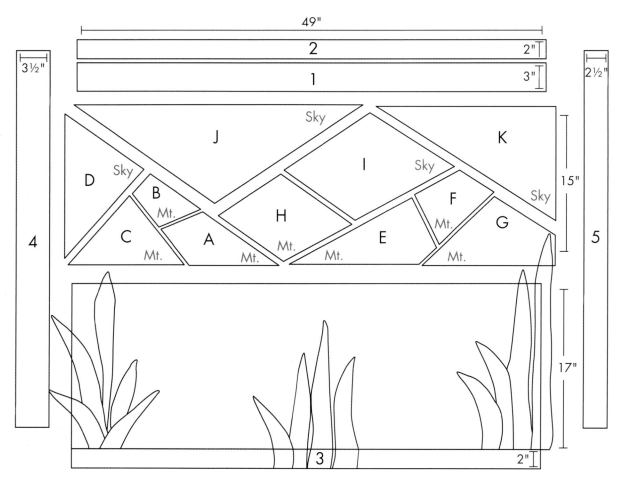

Mountain panel assembly and foliage appliqué placement

Making the Foothills Panel

Join sections A, B, C & D.

Join section E & F, then add G and H.

Join sections I & J. Add to the E/F/G/H unit.

Join the 2 pieced units to complete the Foothills Panel.

Join the Mountain and Foothills panels.

Follow the Mountains Panel assembly diagram to add strips 1 & 2, strip 3, then the side strips 4 and 5 to complete the top.

APPLIQUÉ AND FINISHING

Draw 3 circles of slightly different sizes for the moons. Position them as shown, trim the excess from the 2 moons in the back, and appliqué them to the quilt.

Freehand cut the foliage for foreground interest and appliqué to the quilt.

Quilt as you prefer and bind your quilt.

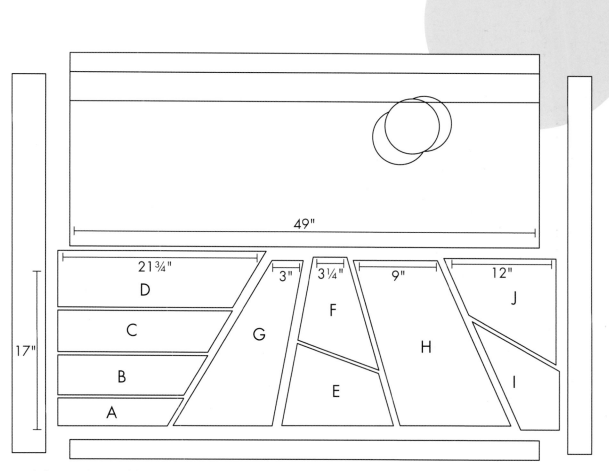

Foothills panel assembly and moon appliqué placement

DREAM TIME

A smaller, simpler version of the essence of a mountain/moon landscape. A small wall quilt this size can make a huge difference in the feeling of a big room.

YARDAGE REQUIREMENTS

Adjust these amounts up or down, depending on whether you decide to make this quilt larger or smaller than the original.

- ▲ 1¼ yards for the sky and binding
- ▲ ½ yard EACH of at least 6 coordinating fabrics for the mountains, moon, foreground (bottom), and side panel
- ▲ ¾ yard of at least 2 coordinating fabrics for the foliage
- ▲ 1½ yards for the strip to divide the right panel from the main panel
- ▲ **Backing:** 1¼ yards
- ▲ **Batting:** 36" x 43"

LEFT AND OPPOSITE: DREAM TIME, 32" x 39", made by the author

EASY BATIK LANDSCAPE QUILTS ▲ PAT BROWN

CONSTRUCTION

Determine the finished size of your quilt. Tape together enough sheets of 1" grid graph paper to make a full-size pattern. Use the measurements on the pattern assembly diagram as a guide for drawing the panels and strips.

Cut out the pattern and use the pieces to cut and label your fabrics (letters for the panel sections and numbers for the strips), being sure to add ¼" seam allowance (see General Instructions, pages 8–11).

To make Panel 1, join sections A & B. Add section C. Join D & E and F & G.

Join the D/E and F/G units and add to the A/B/C unit to complete the panel.

Freehand cut the mountains and trace a moon using the appliqué placement diagram as a guide. Appliqué them onto the Sky Panel.

Join the Sky Panel and Panel 1.

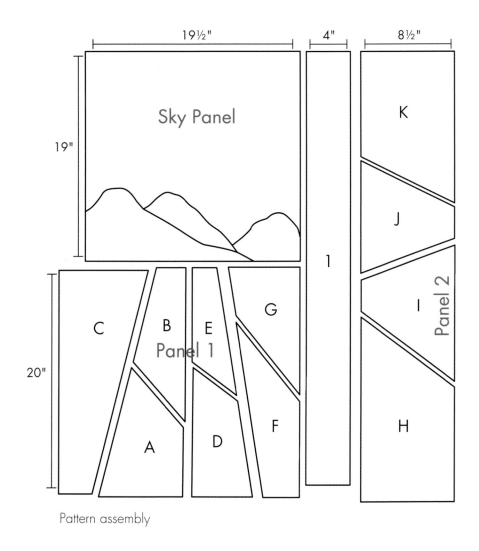

Pattern assembly

Freehand cut foliage and appliqué in place.

Add strip 1 to the right side of the appliquéd panel unit.

To make Panel 2, join sections H & I and J & K. Join the H/I and J/K units to complete the panel.

Freehand cut foliage and appliqué in place.

Add to the previously joined panels to complete the top.

Quilt as you prefer and bind your quilt.

Appliqué placement

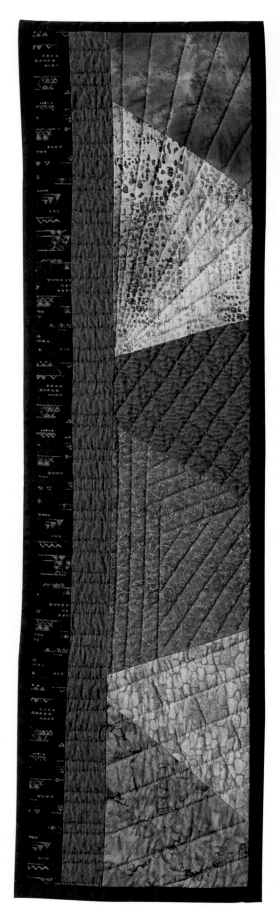
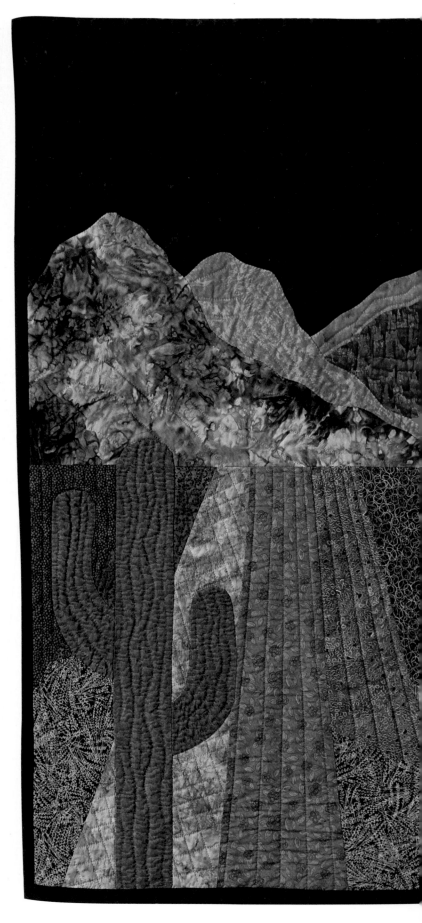

EASY BATIK LANDSCAPE QUILTS ▲ PAT BROWN

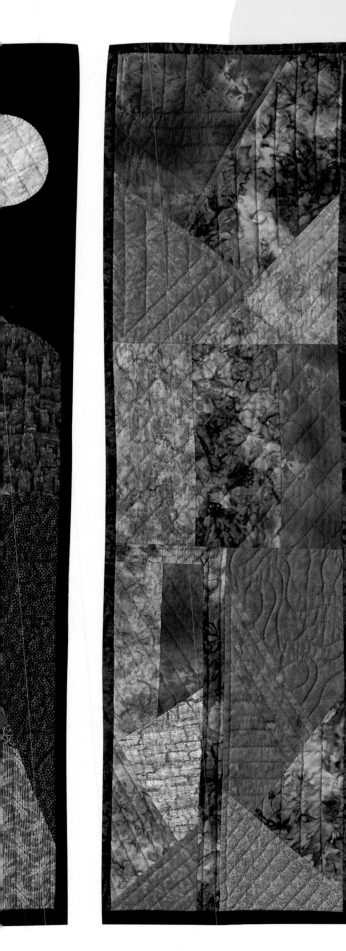

Night Sentinel

There are all kinds of mountains, but when a cactus and a moon are added to the night sky, it truly seems to me to be a Land of Enchantment.

Remember, simplify whenever you want. This can be as simple or as complicated as you wish!

Yardage Requirements

Adjust these amounts up or down, depending on whether you decide to make this quilt larger or smaller than the original.

- ▲ 1½ yards for sky and binding
- ▲ 1½ yards coordinating or contrasting fabric for side strip
- ▲ 1 yard EACH of at least 8 coordinating fabrics for the mountains, pieced foreground, and side panels
- ▲ ¾ yard for the cactus
- ▲ ⅓ yard for the moon
- ▲ **Backing:** 2⅞ yards
- ▲ **Batting:** 2 pieces 17" x 51"
      1 piece 33" x 51"

LEFT: Night Sentinel, 55" x 47", made by the author

CONSTRUCTION

Determine the finished size of your quilt. Tape together enough sheets of 1" grid graph paper to make a full-size pattern. Use the measurements on the pattern assembly diagram as a guide for drawing the panels and strips.

Cut out the pattern and use the pieces to cut and label your fabrics (letters for the panel sections and numbers for the strips), being sure to add ¼" seam allowance (see General Instructions, pages 8–11).

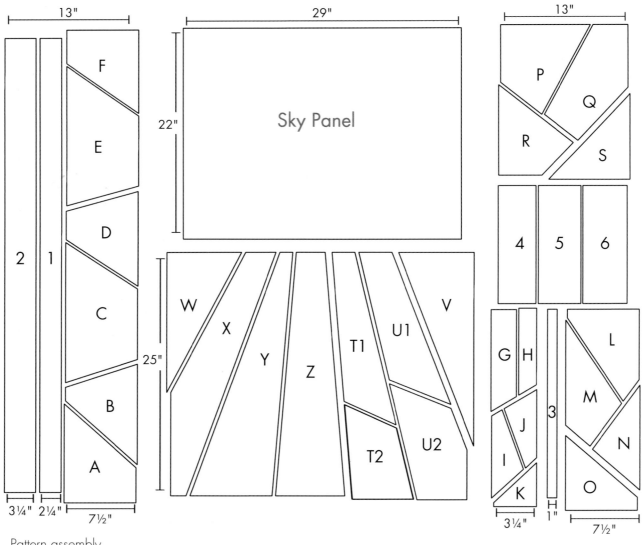

Pattern assembly

Making the Left Panel

Join sections A & B, C & D, and E & F.

Join the A/B unit to the C/D unit. Add the E/F unit to complete the pieced portion.

Add strips 1 & 2 to complete the left panel.

Making the Right Panel

Join sections G & H and I & J.

Join the G/H unit to the I/J unit and add section K.

Join sections L & M. Add section N, then section O.

Join the G/H/I/J/K unit to strip 3, then add the L/M/N/O unit to complete the lower portion of the right panel.

Join sections P & Q. Add section R, then section S to complete the top portion.

Join strips 4, 5 & 6. Add the top and bottom portions to the strip 4/5/6 unit to complete the right panel.

Making the Pieced Center Unit

Join sections T1 & T2 and sections U1 & U2.

Join the T and U units and add section V.

Join sections W & X, Y & Z, then the W/X unit to the Y/Z unit.

Join the T/U/V unit to the W/X/Y/Z unit to complete the center pieced unit.

APPLIQUÉ AND FINISHING

Freehand cut the mountains using the appliqué placement diagram as a guide.

Appliqué the mountains onto the Sky Panel.

Cut a circle for the moon and appliqué in place.

Join the appliquéd Sky Panel to the center pieced unit.

Freehand cut a cactus and appliqué to complete the center panel.

Quilt and bind each panel separately.

Appliqué placement

Moons
NIGHT DANCE

The black background fabric of the night sky really makes the bright colors of the tulips stand out. By making the stems wave and weave around, the tulips look like they are dancing in the moonlight to a song only they can hear!

YARDAGE REQUIREMENTS

Adjust these amounts up or down, depending on whether you decide to make this quilt larger or smaller than the original.

- ▲ 1½ yards black for the night sky
- ▲ ½ yard EACH of at least 3 green fabrics for the pieced panel and foliage
- ▲ 1 yard green fabric for bias tape stems
- ▲ ½ yard EACH of at least 4 coordinating fabrics for moons, tulip petals, and patch
- ▲ **Batting:** 57" x 48"
- ▲ **Backing:** 2¾ yards
- ▲ **Binding:** ⅜ yard

CONSTRUCTION

Determine the finished size of your quilt. Tape together enough sheets of 1" grid graph paper to make a full-size pattern. Use the

RIGHT: NIGHT DANCE, 53" x 44", made by the author

measurements on the pattern assembly diagram as a guide for drawing the panels and strips. Note that any of the sections can be divided for piecing.

Cut out the pattern and use the pieces to cut and label your fabrics (letters for the panel sections and numbers for the strips), being sure to add ¼" seam allowance (see General Instructions, pages 8–11).

Join A & B.

Join C & D, then add to the A/B unit.

Freehand cut a light patch and appliqué in place to complete the pieced panel.

Add to the Sky Panel.

APPLIQUÉ AND FINISHING

Make 3–4 yards of ½" wide bias tape for the stems.

Referring to the appliqué placement diagram, position the stems in gentle curves and appliqué in place.

Using the tulip petal pattern (page 35), cut as many petals as you would like, layer them, and appliqué them at the top of each stem.

Cut 3 small circles and one larger circle for the moons and appliqué in place.

Quilt as you prefer and bind your quilt.

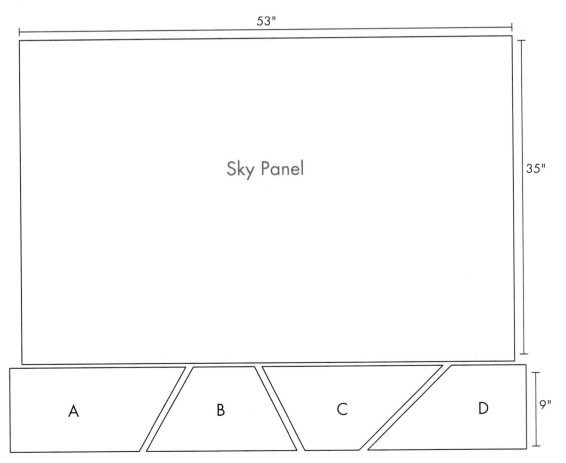

Pattern assembly

Appliqué placement

Tulip Petal Pattern

Enlarge 200%

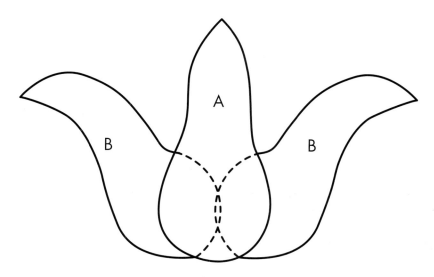

NIGHTFALL...BE VERY CAREFUL

African prints are always such a pleasure to work with. They are very different from the fabrics I usually use. NIGHTFALL...BE VERY CAREFUL transports the mind to the African plain, right next to the mysterious and forbidding nighttime jungle!

YARDAGE REQUIREMENTS

Adjust these amounts up or down, depending on whether you decide to make this quilt larger or smaller than the original.

▲ 2 yards for the sky and binding
▲ 1 yard EACH of at least 7 coordinating fabrics for the panels, foliage, and moons
▲ 1½ yards for the strips between the panels
▲ **Backing:** 2¾ yards
▲ **Batting:** 63" x 49"

LEFT: NIGHTFALL...BE VERY CAREFUL, 59" x 45", made by the author

CONSTRUCTION

Determine the finished size of your quilt. Tape together enough sheets of 1" grid graph paper to make a full-size pattern. Use the measurements on the pattern assembly diagram as a guide for drawing the panels and strips. Note that any of the sections can be divided for piecing.

Cut out the pattern and use the pieces to cut and label your fabrics (letters for the panel sections and numbers for the strips), being sure to add ¼" seam allowance (see General Instructions, pages 8–11).

To make Panel 1, join sections A, B & C.

Trace a moon and freehand cut additional shapes and appliqué in place. Add strips 1 & 2 to complete the panel.

Piece the lower portion of Panel 2 by joining sections D, E, F & G. Freehand cut foliage for the lower left corner and appliqué in place.

Cut out 4 moons, piecing one or more of them as desired. Appliqué to the Sky portion of the panel.

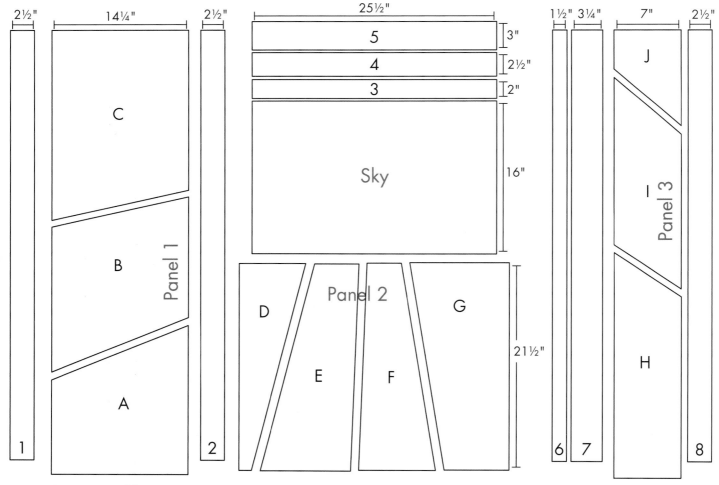

Pattern assembly

Join strips 3, 4 & 5 and add to the Sky.

Add the partially appliquéd lower portion to the Sky section to complete the panel.

Join Panels 1 & 2.

To make Panel 3, join sections H, I & J. Join strips 6 & 7. Add to the left side of the panel. Add strip 8 to the right side to complete the panel.

Join Panel 3 and Panel 2.

Freehand cut foliage and appliqué to the lower right corner of the Panel 2/3 unit.

Join Panel 1 to the Panel 2/3 unit to complete the top.

Quilt as you prefer and bind your quilt.

Embellish with buttons and beads if desired.

Appliqué placement

TOUCH OF DEW

With TOUCH OF DEW the mood is earthy with a dreamy, peaceful feel. A good day is coming to a close and all is right with the world. At least for the moment... and isn't life just millions of moments to embrace or reject?

YARDAGE REQUIREMENTS

Adjust these amounts up or down, depending on whether you decide to make this quilt larger or smaller than the original.

- ▲ 1½ yards main focus fabric
- ▲ 2 yards black for the panels and binding
- ▲ ¾ yard EACH of at least 6 coordinating fabrics for the pieced parts of the panels, foliage, and moons
- ▲ **Backing:** 2¾ yards
- ▲ **Batting:** 60" x 48"

RIGHT: TOUCH OF DEW, 56" x 44", made by the author

CONSTRUCTION

Determine the finished size of your quilt. Tape together enough sheets of 1" grid graph paper to make a full-size pattern. Use the measurements on the pattern assembly diagram as a guide for drawing the panels and strips.

Cut out the pattern and use the pieces to cut and label your fabrics (letters for the panel sections and numbers for the strips), being sure to add ¼" seam allowance (see General Instructions, pages 8–11).

To make Panel 1, join sections A & B. Add strip 1.

Cut out a moon and appliqué in place.

Join strips 3 & 4. Cut out three moons and appliqué in place.

Add strip 2, then join the strip 2/3/4 unit to the Panel 1/strip1 unit.

To make Panel 2, join sections C & D. Add section E to complete the piecing.

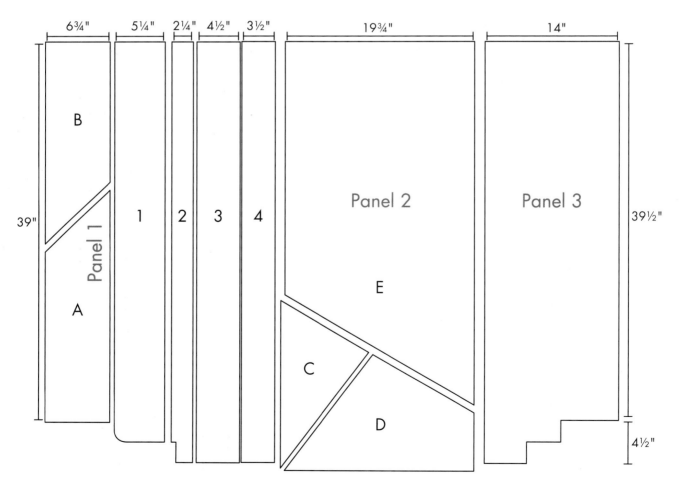

Pattern assembly

Cut out a moon and appliqué in place to complete the panel.

Add to the Panel 1/strips unit.

For Panel 3, freehand cut foliage and one or more abstract shapes and appliqué in place. Add to the right side of the Panel 1/strips/Panel 2 unit to complete the top.

Quilt as preferred and bind your quilt. You'll need to use bias binding to accommodate the curves at the bottom of the quilt. I almost always use black binding as I like the way it frames the piece.

Appliqué placement

Easy BATIK Landscape Quilts ▲ PAT BROWN

SEA MOON

SEA MOON has only two extremely easy quilt blocks set on point—Four-Patch and Square-in-a-Square. The beauty is in the colors and the subject matter of the fabric. This quilt has beautiful sea life represented in the fabric. Be brave and cut off the bottom at different angles to give it a feeling of movement!

YARDAGE REQUIREMENTS

Adjust these amounts up or down, depending on whether you decide to make this quilt larger or smaller than the original.

▲ ½ yard EACH of at least 6 coordinating fabrics for piecing and moon
▲ 1¾ yards coordinating or contrasting fabric for the blocks and binding
▲ **Backing:** 2⅞ yards
▲ **Batting:** 59" x 49"

LEFT: SEA MOON, 55" x 45", made by the author

Sea Moon

CONSTRUCTION

Determine the finished size of your quilt. Adjust the size and/or the number of the blocks according to that size. As shown, the blocks are finished at approximately 15" x 15".

Make 6 Square-in-a-Square blocks, starting with a 10½" x 10½" center square.

Cut 2 – 7¾" x 7¾" squares in half on the diagonal for each block. Add to the 4 sides of the center square to complete the block.

Make 4 Four-Patch blocks with 7½" x 7½" squares. Cut 2 of the blocks in half on the diagonal.

Make a center unit of 2 Four-Patch and 2 Square-in-a-Square blocks set on point. Add the remaining 4 Square-in-a-Square blocks and the diagonally cut Four-Patch blocks. Cut additional triangles to fill in the gaps along the edges.

APPLIQUÉ AND FINISHING

Cut a moon and appliqué it in the upper right-hand corner.

Quilt as you prefer and bind your quilt.

Embellish the moon with beads if desired.

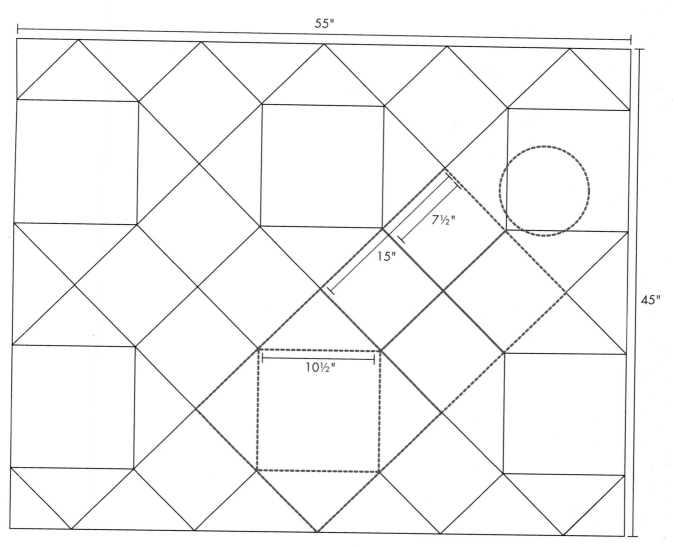

Pattern assembly and appliqué placement

STAR LIGHT...
STAR BRIGHT

This quilt would look terrific in a child's room—in pink for a girl or blue for a boy, of course. This one, they could keep on their wall for many years!

YARDAGE REQUIREMENTS

Adjust these amounts up or down, depending on whether you decide to make this quilt larger or smaller than the original.

▲ 1½ yards main focus fabric for the piecing, star interior border strip, moon, and binding
▲ ¾ yard for the contrasting strip
▲ ½ yard TOTAL of at least 4 coordinating fabrics
▲ **Backing:** 1⅜ yards
▲ **Batting:** 49" x 40"

RIGHT: STAR LIGHT...STAR BRIGHT, 45" x 36", made by the author

CONSTRUCTION

Determine the finished size of your quilt. Tape together enough sheets of 1" grid graph paper to make a full-size pattern. Use the measurements on the pattern assembly and appliqué placement diagram as a guide for drawing the panels and strips.

Piece a Star block of your choice for the lower left corner of the quilt. Notice that you can make it larger than you need and trim off the excess, even if that takes part of the Star.

Cut out the pattern and use the pieces to cut and label your fabrics (letters for the panel sections and numbers for the strips), being sure to add ¼" seam allowance (see General Instructions, pages 8–11).

Add strips 1, 2, 3 & 4 to the Star block, Log-Cabin style.

To make Panel 1, join sections A & B and C & D. Join the A/B and C/D units to complete the panel. Add to the Star block unit.

To make Panel 2, join sections E & F, then join G, H & I. Join the E/F and G/H/I units to complete the panel.

Join Panel 2 and the Star/Panel 1 unit to complete the piecing.

APPLIQUÉ AND FINISHING

Cut a moon, position it as shown, and appliqué in place.

Quilt as you prefer and bind your quilt.

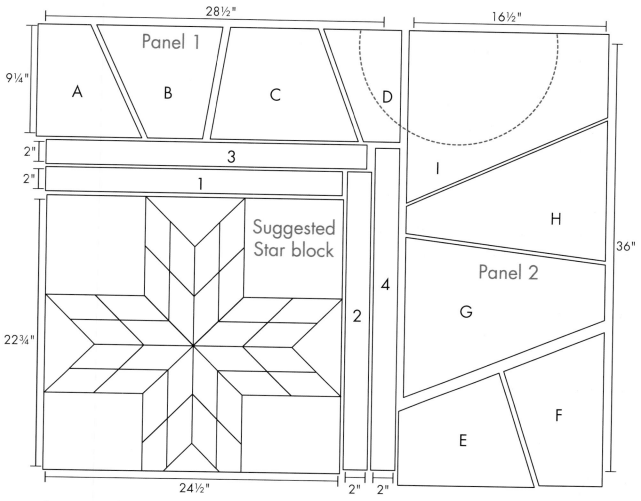

Pattern assembly and appliqué placement

Moods
DESERT MAN

Sometimes it is fun to make a quilt that has an added touch of whimsy. There are many, many suns in this quilt, but where is the man? If you will look very closely, he is dead center at the bottom of the quilt!

YARDAGE REQUIREMENTS

Adjust these amounts up or down, depending on whether you decide to make this quilt larger or smaller than the original.

▲ 1½ yards fabric for main focus fabric for the piecing, strips, and binding

▲ ¾ yard EACH of at least 4 coordinating fabrics for the pieced sections and various strips

▲ ½ yard EACH of at least 2 contrasting fabrics for the suns

▲ **Backing:** 1½ yards

▲ **Batting:** 50" x 43"

RIGHT: DESERT MAN, 46" x 39", made by the author

DESERT MAN

CONSTRUCTION

Determine the finished size of your quilt. Tape together enough sheets of 1" grid graph paper to make a full-size pattern. Use the measurements on the pattern assembly diagram as a guide for drawing the panels and strips.

Cut out the pattern and use the pieces to cut and label your fabrics (letters for the panel sections and numbers for the strips), being sure to add ¼" seam allowance (see General Instructions, pages 8–11).

To make Panel 1, join sections A, B & C. Add strips 1 & 2. Cut out a sun and appliqué in place to complete Panel 1.

To make Panel 2, join sections D & E. Add Section F, then Section G. Add Section H to the D/E/F/G unit. Add section I to complete the panel.

To make Panel 3, join sections J, K & L. Cut out a sun and appliqué in place. Add strip 3 to complete the panel.

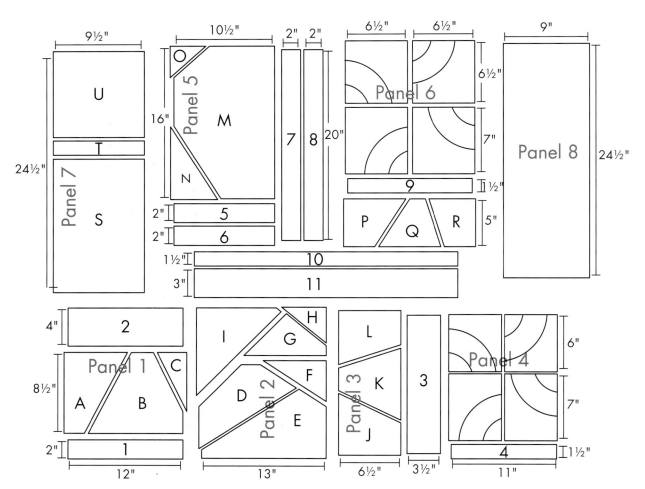

Pattern assembly

To make Panel 4, construct 4 curved-piece blocks. Join in a four-patch unit. Cut 2 suns and appliqué in place. Add strip 4 to complete the panel.

Join Panels 1, 2, 3 & 4.

To make Panel 5, add sections N & O to section M. Join strips 5 & 6 and 7 & 8. Add the 5/6 strip unit to the bottom, then the 7/8 strip unit to the right side. Cut out 4 suns and appliqué in place to complete the panel.

To make Panel 6, join sections P, Q & R. Add strip 9. Construct a curved-piece four-patch unit as you did for Panel 4 and add to the P/Q/R unit. Cut out a sun and appliqué in place.

Join Panels 5 & 6. Join strips 10 & 11 and add to the Panel 5/6 unit.

To make Panel 7, join sections S, T & U. Note that sections S and U can be single pieces of fabric or pieced. Cut out a sun and appliqué in place to complete the panel.

Add to the panel 5/6 unit.

Similarly, Panel 8 can be made with a single piece of fabric or pieced. Add to the Panel 5/6/7 unit. Cut out 2 suns and appliqué in place.

Join the Panel 5/6/7/8 unit to the Panel 1/2/3/4 unit to complete the top.

Quilt as you prefer and bind your quilt.

Appliqué placement

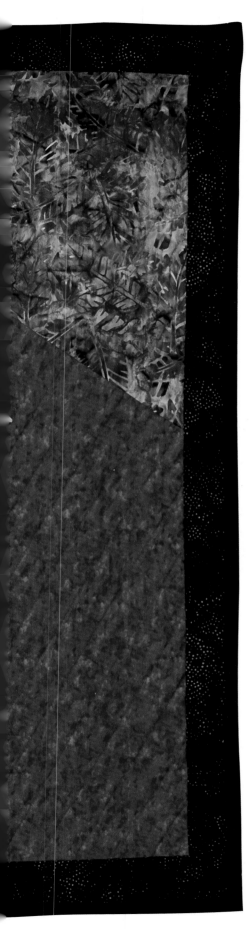

TUSCAN MORNING

TUSCAN MORNING depicts the most heart-felt, cheerful morning. Imagine the perfection of the view from both the inside and the outside of that window!

YARDAGE REQUIREMENTS

Adjust these amounts up or down, depending on whether you decide to make this quilt larger or smaller than the original.

- ▲ 1 yard EACH of at least 5 coordinating fabrics for the pieced panels, mountain, and window arch
- ▲ 1¾ yards EACH of 2 contrasting fabrics for the strips and binding
- ▲ ¾ yard sky fabric
- ▲ ½ yard EACH of at least 4 coordinating fabrics for the flower pot, flowers, table, and sun
- ▲ ½ yard green for bias stems
- ▲ **Backing:** 2⅞ yards
- ▲ **Batting:** 56" x 51"

LEFT: TUSCAN MORNING, 52" x 47", made by the author

CONSTRUCTION

Determine the finished size of your quilt. Tape together enough sheets of 1" grid graph paper to make a full-size pattern. Use the measurements on the pattern assembly diagram as a guide for drawing the panels and strips.

Cut out the pattern and use the pieces to cut and label your fabrics (letters for the panel sections and numbers for the strips), being sure to add ¼" seam allowance (see General Instructions, pages 8–11).

To make Panel 1, join sections A, B & C. Join strips 1, 2 & 3. Join the strip 1/2/3 unit with the A/B/C unit to complete the panel.

Freehand cut a mountain and appliqué it to the base of the Sky Panel.

Freehand cut a window arch and appliqué it in place.

Add strip 4 to complete the Sky Panel.

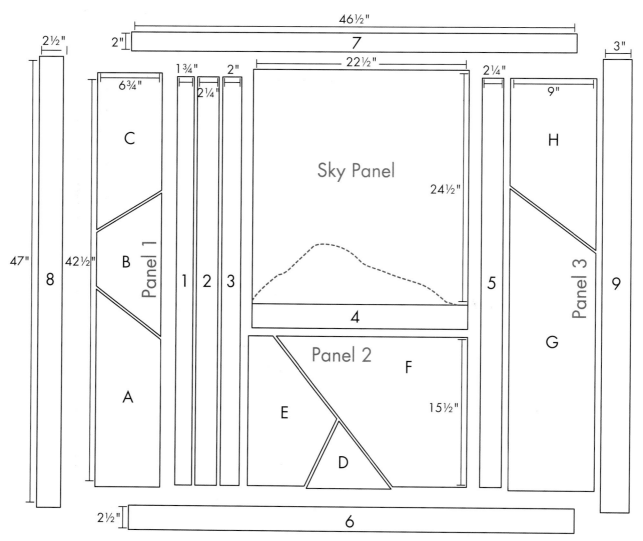

Pattern assembly

To make Panel 2, join sections D & E. Freehand cut a table for the flower pot and appliqué it to section F. Freehand cut a flower pot and appliqué it in place, leaving the top of the vase open so you can tuck in the flower stems later.

Add section F to the E/D unit to complete Panel 2.

Join Panel 2 and the Sky Panel. Add strip 5.

Make bias stems with the green fabric and appliqué in place. Finish appliquéing the top of the vase.

Freehand cut 11 or more flower petals and appliqué them onto the stems.

To make Panel 3, join sections G & H. Join with the 1/2/Sky Panel unit.

Add strips 6 & 7 to the top and bottom. Add strips 8 & 9 to the sides to complete the top.

Quilt as you prefer and bind your quilt.

Appliqué placement

TROPICAL MORNING

Using tropical blues in a wall landscape quilt truly makes a special statement. An entire room could be decorated around a quilt such as this! Adding pillows made with these same colors can make a room come alive with a tropical mood.

YARDAGE REQUIREMENTS

Adjust these amounts up or down, depending on whether you decide to make this quilt larger or smaller than the original.

- ▲ 1¾ yards EACH of at least 2 blue tropical fabrics for the panels, strips, and binding
- ▲ 1½ yards EACH of at least 5 coordinating fabrics for the panels, palm trees, contrasting strips, suns, and coral
- ▲ ¼ yard EACH of at least 2 greens for the palm trees
- ▲ **Backing:** 2¾ yards
- ▲ **Batting:** 62" x 50"

RIGHT: TROPICAL MORNING, 58" x 46", made by the author

CONSTRUCTION

Determine the finished size of your quilt. Tape together enough sheets of 1" grid graph paper to make a full-size pattern. Use the measurements on the pattern assembly diagram as a guide for drawing the panels and strips. Note that any of the sections can be divided for piecing.

Cut out the pattern and use the pieces to cut and label your fabrics (letters for the panel sections and numbers for the strips), being sure to add ¼" seam allowance (see General Instructions, pages 8–11).

To make Panel 1, join sections A, B & C. Add strip 1.

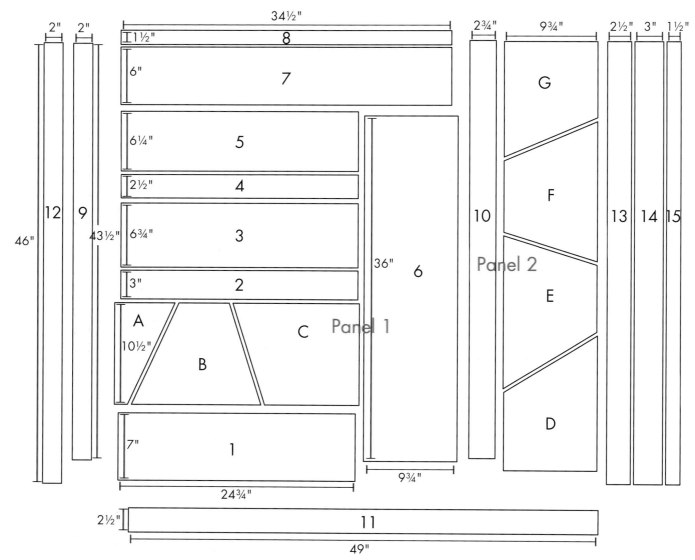

Pattern assembly

Join strips 2 & 3, 4 & 5, and 7 & 8. Join the 2/3 unit with the 4/5 unit and add to the A/B/C/strip 1 unit.

Add strip 6, the strip 7/8 unit, and strip 9 to complete Panel 1.

Freehand cut pieces for the coral and appliqué in place.

Cut out 2 suns and appliqué them in place.

To make Panel 2, join sections D & E and F & G. Join the D/E & F/G units. Add strip 10 to complete the panel.

Join Panels 1 & 2. Add strip 11 and 12. Join strips 13, 14 & 15 and add to complete the top.

Freehand cut 2 palm tree trunks and appliqué them in place.

Freehand cut 8 or more palm fronds and appliqué to the palm tree trunks to complete the top.

Quilt as you prefer and bind your quilt.

Appliqué placement

Country Lights/City Lights

These two small landscapes are all about color combinations. The CITY LIGHTS colors pick up the sophisticated colors of the city where COUNTRY LIGHTS colors are the more humble earth tones. Either one could make a small space very special!

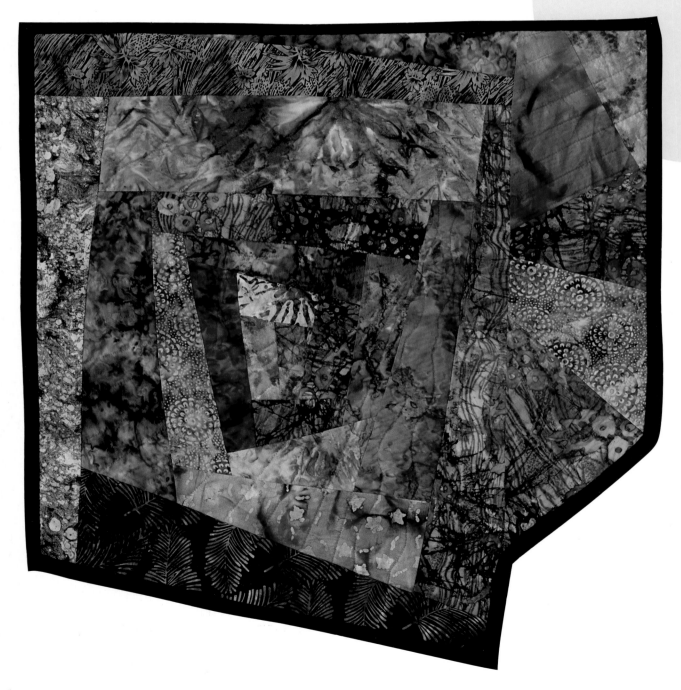

OPPOSITE: CITY LIGHTS, approximately 30" x 36", made by the author

ABOVE: COUNTRY LIGHTS, approximately 30" x 36", made by the author

ABOVE: CITY LIGHTS, detail. Full quilt on page 64.

YARDAGE REQUIREMENTS

Adjust these amounts up or down, depending on whether you decide to make this quilt larger or smaller than the original.

- ▲ 1 yard of focus fabric for piecing and binding
- ▲ 1 yard EACH of 2 coordinating fabrics
- ▲ ½ yard EACH of at least 3 coordinating fabrics for piecing
- ▲ **Backing:** 1¼ yards
- ▲ **Batting:** 34" x 40"

CONSTRUCTION

Determine the finished size of your quilt. Although a pattern is provided, consider doing either (or both) of these quilts completely freeform instead of making a pattern. Note that any of the sections can be pieced.

Start with a center piece (D) and just keep adding strips of various widths Log-Cabin style, as indicated on the pattern assembly diagram. When the approximate size you want is achieved, cut the main panel using the diagram as a guide.

Piece a second panel and sew to the main panel.

Trim the bottom edge at an interesting angle.

Quilt as you prefer and bind your quilt.

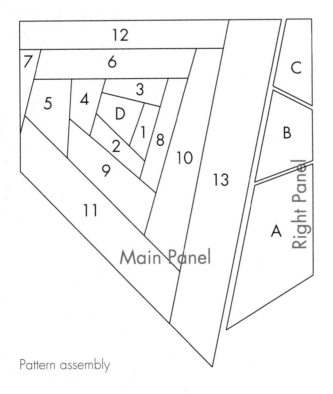

Pattern assembly

Winding Path

WINDING PATH is a little gem that can be done quickly. The path is simply yarn curved around and tacked to the quilt—an example of something small having a big impact.

Yardage Requirements

Adjust these amounts up or down, depending on whether you decide to make this quilt larger or smaller than the original.

- ▲ 1 yard for the side strip, piecing, and binding
- ▲ ½ yard EACH of at least 4 coordinating fabrics for the piecing, sun, and patches
- ▲ **Backing:** 1 yard
- ▲ **Batting:** 27" x 33"

Construction

Determine the finished size of your quilt. Tape together enough sheets of 1" grid graph paper to make a full-size pattern. Use the measurements on the pattern assembly diagram as a guide for drawing the panels and strips.

RIGHT: WINDING PATH, detail. Full quilt on page 68.

ABOVE: WINDING PATH, 23" x 29", made by the author

Cut out the pattern and use the pieces to cut and label your fabrics (letters for the panel sections and numbers for the strips), being sure to add ¼" seam allowance (see General Instructions, pages 8–11).

To make Panel 1, join sections A & B and add C to complete the panel.

To make Panel 2, join sections D & E. Add section F, then G. Cut a sun and appliqué in place to complete the panel.

Join Panels 1 & 2.

To make Panel 3 as shown, join 20 squares into 4 rows of 5 squares each. Freehand cut a patch and appliqué along the right-hand edge. You can vary the number and size of the squares any way you like.

Join Panel 3 to the Panel 1/2 unit.

Freehand cut a patch and appliqué along the left edge. Add strip 1 to the right-hand edge to complete the top.

Quilt as you prefer and bind your quilt.

Use a decorative yarn to create a path and tack in place. Embellish the quilt with beads if desired.

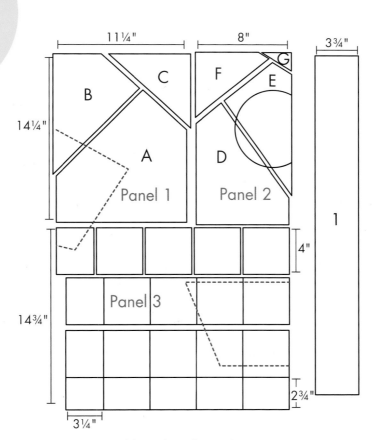

Pattern assembly and appliqué placement

PERFECT ENDING

There are very few things as beautiful as a perfect sunset. To be on a sailboat to witness it has to be the perfect ending to a perfect day!

YARDAGE REQUIREMENTS

Adjust these amounts up or down, depending on whether you decide to make this quilt larger or smaller than the original.

- ▲ 1¾ yards EACH of at least 2 coordinating fabrics for strips, panel piecing, and binding
- ▲ ½ yard EACH of at least 3 coordinating fabrics for panel piecing
- ▲ 1¼ yards for the sky
- ▲ ⅓ yard for the sun
- ▲ Use some of these fabrics for the clouds, sailboat, and patches
- ▲ **Backing:** 2½ yards
- ▲ **Batting:** 59" x 44"

RIGHT: PERFECT ENDING, 55" x 40", made by the author

CONSTRUCTION

Determine the finished size of your quilt. Tape together enough sheets of 1" grid graph paper to make a full-size pattern. Use the measurements on the pattern assembly diagram as a guide for drawing the panels and strips.

Cut out the pattern and use the pieces to cut and label your fabrics (letters for the panel sections and numbers for the strips), being sure to add ¼" seam allowance (see General Instructions, pages 8–11).

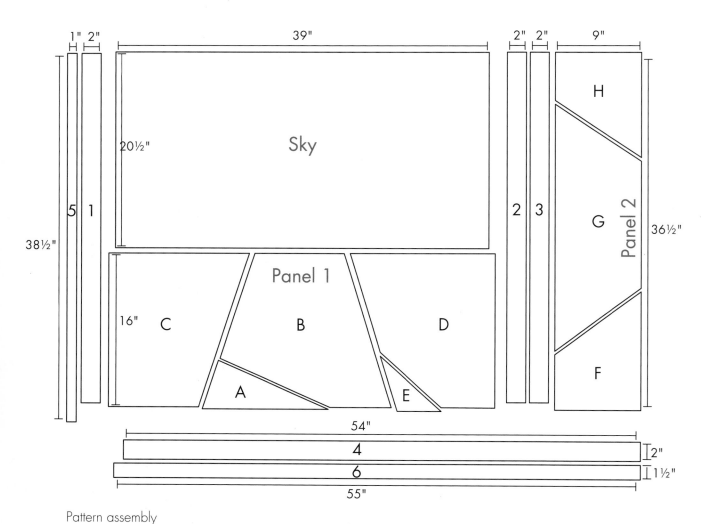

Pattern assembly

To make Panel 1, join sections A & B and add C. Join D & E and add to the A/B/C unit.

Cut a sun and freehand cut 2 clouds and appliqué to the Sky portion.

Join the Sky to the A/B/C/D unit. Add strip 1 to complete the panel.

To make Panel 2, join sections F, G & H. Join strips 2 & 3 and add to the F/G/H unit to complete the panel.

Join the 2 panels. Add strips 4, 5 & 6 Log-Cabin style to complete the top.

Freehand cut a sailboat, mast, and sail and appliqué to the lower portion of the quilt.

Piece patch 1 and freehand cut patches 2 & 3. Position as desired onto the quilt and appliqué in place.

Quilt as you prefer and bind your quilt.

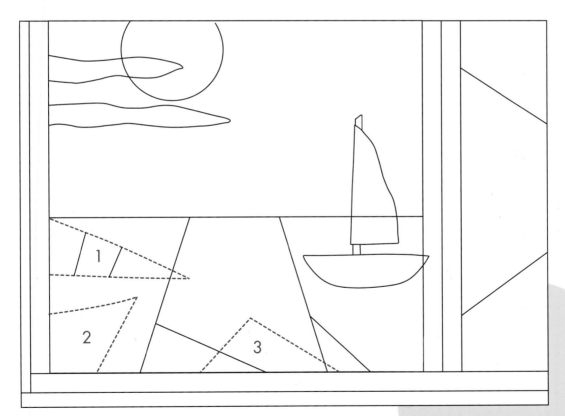

Appliqué placement

Gallery

Easy BATIK Landscape Quilts ▲ PAT BROWN

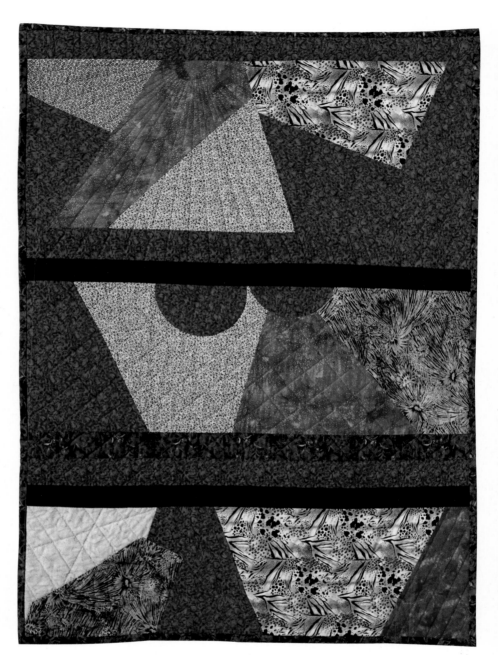

LEFT: EVENING WHISPER, 57" x 46", made by the author.
EVENING WHISPER brings all the colors together to put on a perfect show of colors. If you ever have wanted to go wild with colors, now is your chance!

ABOVE: SCARLET MOON, 42" x 56", made by the author.
Putting African prints with reds is a great combination. If you have a very boring spot in any room, a quilt in these colors will liven up the spot in a hurry!

ABOVE: SUMMER DELIGHT, 46" x 46", made by the author.
SUMMER DELIGHT puts us in an August garden when the flowers are at their
very best. The sun is shining down and, at that moment, all that weeding
was worth it.

ABOVE: DID YOU SEE THE SUNRISE THIS MORNING?, 33" x 51" and 18" x 51", made by the author. One of the best treats in the world is to start each day with a beautiful sunrise. Those people who live in climates that allow them to view a sight such as this almost every morning are truly the luckiest people in the world.

QUILTING SUGGESTIONS

I use the same quilting patterns over and over again on my landscape quilts. The mountains almost always are quilted with wavy lines. It gives them a layered look. Wavy lines placed randomly across the sky work well, too.

I use a lot of straight lines, marked with a yardstick. I'll create a checkerboard pattern by placing straight lines perpendicular to the first set of lines.

Moonbeams and sun rays are quilted in radiating lines out from the sphere.

NIGHT SENTINEL (pages 28–29 and featured here) shows the basic techniques that I use most often. I have found that using a small-scale checkerboard pattern on the moon or sun makes it appear almost three-dimensional.

Simple lines can make an intricate quilting pattern that is actually very easy to do!

ABOUT THE AUTHOR

I began my quilting journey in 1978 very reluctantly! A good friend kept trying to get me to go with her for quilting lessons and I kept putting her off. I thought I didn't have enough interest. She finally wore me down and from the first lesson I found I couldn't get enough!

I made samplers, Amish-style quilts, and traditional quilts, as everyone did back then. As time went on, I lost interest in the same old fabrics.

I had a second son and that pretty much stopped my quilting life for many years. I've always been a stay-at-home mom, so when the last son left home, I had lots of time on my hands. I visited a quilt shop in Indianapolis, saw the batik fabrics, and fell in love all over again!

Batiks have opened up a whole new world to me. All kinds of designs keep dancing in my head. I loved putting together all the different color combinations that are so uniquely batik. "Naturescapes" is how I think of my designs. Using basic techniques and beautiful fabrics, a traditional quilter can easily become an art quilter.

Come visit me at: www.quiltedmoon.com

Pat Brown

MORE AQS BOOKS

This is only a small selection of the books available from the American Quilter's Society. AQS books are known worldwide for timely topics, clear writing, beautiful color photos, and accurate illustrations and patterns. The following books are available from your local bookseller, quilt shop, or public library.

#8532

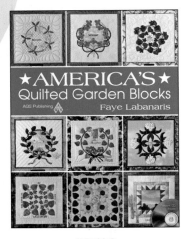

#8530

#8523

#8531

#8525

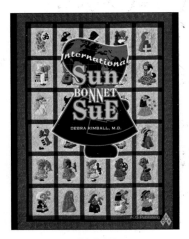

#8347

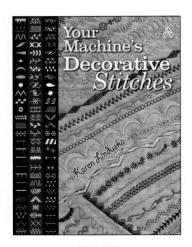

#8353

#8355

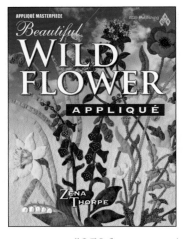

#8526